SPELLING PRACTICE YEAR 4

THIS BOOK BELONGS TO

WHiZ
KiD
BOOKS

Spelling Practice Year 4 by Whiz Kid Books

Published by Alterra Business Consulting Ltd

Copyright © 2023 Whiz Kid Books

Tips for Spelling Practice

Thank you for purchasing the Spelling Practice Year 4 workbook.

There are 72 lessons with a total of 576 words. Each page contains 8 words for your child to learn. Some children will learn more quickly than others so it is important to work at the right pace for your child. Little and often is the best way to help them succeed.

Start by working together. Ask your child to:
- Read the word (help them if necessary)
- Learn the letters by repeating them out loud
- Copy the word, saying the letters out loud
- Remember the word, cover with a sheet of paper and write the word in the final column. See below.
- Check all the spellings and put a score in the box at the bottom of the page.

Lesson 1		
Read & Learn	Copy	Cover & Write
high	high	
every		
near		
west		

Lesson 1		
Read & Learn	Copy	Cover & Write

Finally, at the bottom of the page is a list of words. Ask your child to circle the ones which are spelled correctly.

CIRCLE THE CORRECT SPELLINGS	SCORE
else dres neer high	8
netx west every besst	

Lesson 1

Read & Learn	Copy	Cover & Write
high		
every		
near		
west		
dress		
best		
next		
else		

CIRCLE THE CORRECT SPELLINGS

high best esel dress

weste neer every next

SCORE

/8

Lesson 2

Read & Learn	Copy	Cover & Write
checked		
grand		
stand		
am		
matter		
forms		
value		
area		

CIRCLE THE CORRECT SPELLINGS

aree forms mater checked

grand stande am valeu

/8

netx   west   every   besst

Lesson 3

Read & Learn	Copy	Cover & Write
between		
own		
base		
country		
plant		
slip		
lunch		
pond		

CIRCLE THE CORRECT SPELLINGS

between pnod own contry

slip lunhc plant base

SCORE

/8

Lesson 4

Read & Learn	Copy	Cover & Write
front		
thump		
inches		
yard		
stored		
motion		
expand		
calculate		

CIRCLE THE CORRECT SPELLINGS

calulate front thump yadr

inches stord motion espand

SCORE

/ 8

Lesson 5

Read & Learn	Copy	Cover & Write
save		
school		
father		
keep		
safe		
grade		
reached		
raise		

CIRCLE THE CORRECT SPELLINGS

raise safe graed reached

skool farther keep save

SCORE

/8

Lesson 6

Read & Learn	Copy	Cover & Write
theme		
scream		
easy		
batteries		
fuel		
iron		
solve		
science		

CIRCLE THE CORRECT SPELLINGS

theem   scream   eesy   solve

sience   iron   feul   batterees

SCORE

/8

Lesson 7

Read & Learn	Copy	Cover & Write
trade		
start		
city		
earth		
hope		
stone		
follow		
broke		

CIRCLE THE CORRECT SPELLINGS

brock trade sity start

folloe stone hope erth

SCORE

/8

Lesson 8

Read & Learn	Copy	Cover & Write
sign		
tiny		
whole		
waves		
current		
electric		
digit		
round		

CIRCLE THE CORRECT SPELLINGS

sine tiny round diggit

waves ellectric whole currant

SCORE

/8

Lesson 9

Read & Learn	Copy	Cover & Write
upon		
thought		
gun		
strong		
story		
burst		
strip		
stream		

CIRCLE THE CORRECT SPELLINGS

else   dres   neer   high

netx   west   every   besst

SCORE

⎯⎯ / 8

Lesson 10

Read & Learn	Copy	Cover & Write
street		
distance		
least		
hundred		
east		
object		
sum		
difference		

CIRCLE THE CORRECT SPELLINGS

SCORE

strete leest distance eest

sum diference hundred oject

/8

Lesson 11

Read & Learn	Copy	Cover & Write
cried		
dried		
milk		
let's		
while		
known		
knife		
knock		

CIRCLE THE CORRECT SPELLINGS

knock nife dryed wile

cried lets knoun milk

SCORE

/8

Lesson 12

Read & Learn	Copy	Cover & Write
wrong		
knot		
wrinkle		
wrap		
wrist		
knee		
product		
quotient		

CIRCLE THE CORRECT SPELLINGS

product nee qotient rap

wrinkle knott wrong wirst

SCORE

/8

Lesson 13

Read & Learn	Copy	Cover & Write
along		
bought		
close		
something		
seem		
laughed		
lady		
enough		

CIRCLE THE CORRECT SPELLINGS

seem somthing lady close

allong enuff bought laughed

SCORE

/8

Lesson 14

Read & Learn	Copy	Cover & Write
graph		
paragraph		
photograph		
particle		
atom		
element		
decimal		
property		

CIRCLE THE CORRECT SPELLINGS

SCORE

parragraph particle atom deiicmal

ellement photograph graph

/8

Lesson 15

Read & Learn	Copy	Cover & Write
cloud		
child		
open		
example		
begin		
change		
match		
watch		

CIRCLE THE CORRECT SPELLINGS

SCORE

wach open example beggin

match change clod child

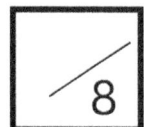

Lesson 16

Read & Learn	Copy	Cover & Write
steel		
speech		
source		
direction		
travel		
women		
demonstrate		
batch		

CIRCLE THE CORRECT SPELLINGS

batch speach source travle

steel directoin women

SCORE

/8

Lesson 17

Read & Learn	Copy	Cover & Write
can't		
shall		
those		
both		
paper		
pushed		
sharp		
shock		

CIRCLE THE CORRECT SPELLINGS

paper bath cant shart

pushed shokc shall thoose

SCORE

/8

Lesson 18

Read & Learn	Copy	Cover & Write
crash		
showed		
shoes		
shadows		
reflect		
mirror		
fraction		
determine		

CIRCLE THE CORRECT SPELLINGS

SCORE

determine   crash   shadouws

shoos   reflact   mirror

/8

Lesson 19

Read & Learn	Copy	Cover & Write
together		
tied		
group		
often		
table		
space		
fence		
price		

CIRCLE THE CORRECT SPELLINGS

tabel tied prise space

often groop together

SCORE

/8

Lesson 20

Read & Learn	Copy	Cover & Write
office		
police		
pencil		
civil		
survive		
behaviour		
dance		
fact		

CIRCLE THE CORRECT SPELLINGS

fakt police pensil survive

sivil behavior office

/8

Lesson 21

Read & Learn	Copy	Cover & Write
important		
cannot		
children		
wife		
hoe		
giraffe		
gentle		
stage		

CIRCLE THE CORRECT SPELLINGS

hoe   important   childern   wife

stage   girafe   canot

SCORE

/8

Lesson 22

Read & Learn	Copy	Cover & Write
engine		
badge		
ginger		
ocean		
desert		
tundra		
equation		
operation		

CIRCLE THE CORRECT SPELLINGS

SCORE

dessert badge operatoin ocean

tundra eqation enginne

/8

Lesson 23

Read & Learn	Copy	Cover & Write
held		
cross		
night		
walk		
picked		
choice		
voice		
royal		

CIRCLE THE CORRECT SPELLINGS

held cros royal chioce

walk vioce night picked

SCORE

/8

Lesson 24

Read & Learn	Copy	Cover & Write
annoy		
noise		
destroy		
forest		
grassland		
wetland		
wild		
relationship		

CIRCLE THE CORRECT SPELLINGS

forrest noise wettland

destroy wild anoy grasland

SCORE

/8

Lesson 25

Read & Learn	Copy	Cover & Write
sea		
began		
shouted		
took		
river		
crown		
howevez		
around		

CIRCLE THE CORRECT SPELLINGS

took see shouted rivver

howevre arround crown began

/8

Lesson 26

Read & Learn	Copy	Cover & Write
growl		
fountain		
ground		
pounds		
beneficial		
influence		
multiplication		
division		

CIRCLE THE CORRECT SPELLINGS

grolw ground influense pounds

multiplcation division fountain

Lesson 27

Read & Learn	Copy	Cover & Write
sleep		
carry		
north		
once		
book		
crawl		
laundry		
author		

CIRCLE THE CORRECT SPELLINGS

laundry slepe north book

crawl cary awthor once

/8

Lesson 28

Read & Learn	Copy	Cover & Write
taught		
pause		
dawn		
extinct		
resemble		
disappear		
polygon		
integer		

CIRCLE THE CORRECT SPELLINGS

tawght plygon ressemble dawn

extinct pawse disappear

SCORE

/ 8

Lesson 29

Read & Learn	Copy	Cover & Write
south		
sir		
without		
second		
birds		
loose		
choose		
shook		

CIRCLE THE CORRECT SPELLINGS

choose sir sowth loose

shoke second without birds

SCORE

/8

Lesson 30

Read & Learn	Copy	Cover & Write
understood		
balloon		
locked		
predict		
pattern		
season		
pentagon		
hexagon		

CIRCLE THE CORRECT SPELLINGS

predict hexxagon seeson locked

baloon pattern understood

SCORE

/8

Lesson 31

Read & Learn	Copy	Cover & Write
miss		
idea		
copy		
poor		
floor		
started		
stars		
carpet		

CIRCLE THE CORRECT SPELLINGS

stars idea pore floor

carrpet miss copey miss

SCORE

/8

Lesson 32

Read & Learn	Copy	Cover & Write
marker		
party		
pardon		
lunar		
cycle		
appearance		
octagon		
classify		

CIRCLE THE CORRECT SPELLINGS

octogon marker parrdon lunar

cycle party clasify

Lesson 33

Read & Learn	Copy	Cover & Write
among		
buy		
Indian		
real		
almost		
stairs		
airplane		
compare		

CIRCLE THE CORRECT SPELLINGS

SCORE

compare allmost among buy

Indian stiars airplane real

/8

Lesson 34

Read & Learn	Copy	Cover & Write
glare		
repair		
prepare		
attributes		
quadrilateral		
isosceles		
equilateral		
scalene		

CIRCLE THE CORRECT SPELLINGS

issoceles scalene glare repare

equilateral preparre atributes

SCORE

Lesson 35

Read & Learn	Copy	Cover & Write
fly		
born		
smell		
sometimes		
mountains		
worn		
fourth		
war		

CIRCLE THE CORRECT SPELLINGS

warr smell sometimes woen

mountains fouht born fly

SCORE

/8

Lesson 36

Read & Learn	Copy	Cover & Write
horse		
morning		
poured		
geometric		
angles		
acute		
obtuse		
blood		

CIRCLE THE CORRECT SPELLINGS

SCORE

/ 8

blod horse pored obtuse

morning acute geommtric angles

Lesson 37

Read & Learn	Copy	Cover & Write
verb		
young		
talk		
pulled		
list		
here		
hear		
bare		

CIRCLE THE CORRECT SPELLINGS

verb here hear barre talk

list yuong pulled

Lesson 38

Read & Learn	Copy	Cover & Write
bear		
way		
weigh		
telescope		
magnify		
planets		
pyramid		
cone		

CIRCLE THE CORRECT SPELLINGS

piramid   wiegh   planets   bear

mangify   way   cone   telescope

SCORE

/8

Lesson 39

Read & Learn	Copy	Cover & Write
sugar		
being		
leave		
noun		
it's		
flower		
flour		
bored		

CIRCLE THE CORRECT SPELLINGS

it's beeing nown flour

shugar leave bored flowers

SCORE

/8

Lesson 40

Read & Learn	Copy	Cover & Write
board		
hair		
hare		
clear		
orbit		
position		
sphere		
vet		

CIRCLE THE CORRECT SPELLINGS

cleer vett hare orbit

board possition hair spheer

/8

Lesson 41

Read & Learn	Copy	Cover & Write
perfect		
curled		
church		
firm		
skirt		
clerk		
shirt		
person		

CIRCLE THE CORRECT SPELLINGS

skirt personn clerk church

perfect shirt firm curld

/8

Lesson 42

Read & Learn	Copy	Cover & Write
terms		
jerked		
burned		
conduct		
experiment		
observation		
prism		
cylinder		

CIRCLE THE CORRECT SPELLINGS

cininder jerked experiment

obsertion prisum terms buned

SCORE

/8

Lesson 43

Read & Learn	Copy	Cover & Write
hugged		
correct		
funny		
happy		
puppy		
common		
collect		
bottles		

CIRCLE THE CORRECT SPELLINGS

common funy puppy colect

bottles happey correct hugged

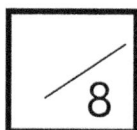

Lesson 44

Read & Learn	Copy	Cover & Write
different		
lesson		
error		
evidence		
conclusion		
opinion		
certain		
likely		

CIRCLE THE CORRECT SPELLINGS

SCORE

conllusion likely diferent evidense

error opinion lesson certian

/8

Lesson 45

Read & Learn	Copy	Cover & Write
thick		
strangest		
bigger		
better		
higher		
tallest		
richest		
smarter		

CIRCLE THE CORRECT SPELLINGS

highter tallest thick biger

better smarker richst strangest

SCORE

/8

Lesson 46

Read & Learn	Copy	Cover & Write
louder		
hotter		
jumped		
describe		
data		
farmers		
unlikely		
visit		

CIRCLE THE CORRECT SPELLINGS

visit jumped descibe data

unlikely loudre farmers hoter

Lesson 47

Read & Learn	Copy	Cover & Write
notebook		
sunset		
bookcase		
classroom		
everyone		
football		
sunshine		
rainbow		

CIRCLE THE CORRECT SPELLINGS

SCORE

clasroom shunshone sunsett

notebook rainbow evryone

$\boxed{/8}$

Lesson 48

Read & Learn	Copy	Cover & Write
baseball		
hallway		
outdoors		
measurement		
numeral		
outcome		
future		
forecast		

CIRCLE THE CORRECT SPELLINGS

SCORE

numeral forcast basebal hallway

outdoors outcom future

/8

Lesson 49

Read & Learn	Copy	Cover & Write
winter		
army		
cellar		
garden		
market		
basket		
welcome		
until		

CIRCLE THE CORRECT SPELLINGS

SCORE

untill army winter celar

basket garden markit wlecome

/8

Lesson 50

Read & Learn	Copy	Cover & Write
always		
cowboy		
lasso		
logical		
continuity		
change		
estimate		
whose		

CIRCLE THE CORRECT SPELLINGS

always estimat whoose lasso

cowboy contunity logical change

SCORE

/8

Lesson 51

Read & Learn	Copy	Cover & Write
cabin		
rule		
music		
tiger		
behind		
rewind		
focus		
belong		

CIRCLE THE CORRECT SPELLINGS

behind tifgre cabin rewind

blong foccus music rule

Lesson 52

Read & Learn	Copy	Cover & Write
family		
brother		
motel		
connect		
local		
strategy		
complex		
diagram		

CIRCLE THE CORRECT SPELLINGS

diagram motel bruther complex

conect fammily strategy diagram

Lesson 53

Read & Learn	Copy	Cover & Write
liked		
worried		
rolling		
singing		
swimming		
settled		
talked		
hurried		

CIRCLE THE CORRECT SPELLINGS

talked woried rolling setled

swimming huried liked singing

SCORE

/8

Lesson 54

Read & Learn	Copy	Cover & Write
buying		
trying		
leaving		
regional		
national		
traditional		
chart		
symbol		

CIRCLE THE CORRECT SPELLINGS

traditional trying chartt simbol

national leeving bying regional

SCORE

/8

Lesson 55

Read & Learn	Copy	Cover & Write
permission		
confession		
vision		
please		
action		
quotation		
hunting		
nation		

CIRCLE THE CORRECT SPELLINGS

action nasion permision please

hunting quotation confesion vision

SCORE

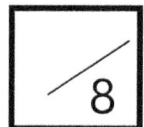

Lesson 56

Read & Learn	Copy	Cover & Write
combination		
question		
attention		
geography		
physical		
divided		
exact		
agreed		

CIRCLE THE CORRECT SPELLINGS

SCORE

agred question atention physical

geography dividid exact

/8

Lesson 57

Read & Learn	Copy	Cover & Write
beautiful		
cheerful		
harmful		
playful		
useful		
colorful		
thankfully		
joyfully		

CIRCLE THE CORRECT SPELLINGS

useful betifful thankfuly joyfully

cheerful harmfil colorful playful

SCORE

/8

Lesson 58

Read & Learn	Copy	Cover & Write
helpfully		
painfully		
stressful		
feature		
crops		
lifted		
advantage		
history		

CIRCLE THE CORRECT SPELLINGS

corps lifted history painfuly

helpfully stresful advantage featur

Lesson 59

Read & Learn	Copy	Cover & Write
lonely		
suddenly		
actually		
personally		
especially		
formally		
rapidly		
dangerously		

CIRCLE THE CORRECT SPELLINGS

SCORE

formaly sudenly actially lonely

rapidly personally eepecially

/8

Lesson 60

Read & Learn	Copy	Cover & Write
tenderly		
lovely		
nicely		
identity		
culture		
society		
accurate		
precise		

CIRCLE THE CORRECT SPELLINGS

lovely cultur siociety precise

tenderly niceley identity accurate

SCORE

/8

Lesson 61

Read & Learn	Copy	Cover & Write
comfortable		
honorably		
erasable		
available		
portable		
laughable		
irritably		
feeling		

CIRCLE THE CORRECT SPELLINGS

SCORE

honorably erasable laghable iritably

feeling comfortable availble

/8

Lesson 62

Read & Learn	Copy	Cover & Write
capable		
disposable		
reusable		
tube		
government		
tribal		
derive		
general		

CIRCLE THE CORRECT SPELLINGS

derive cappable tube trible

genneral disposible reusable

SCORE

/8

Lesson 63

Read & Learn	Copy	Cover & Write
penny		
pennies		
empty		
emptied		
parties		
families		
mystery		
mysteries		

CIRCLE THE CORRECT SPELLINGS

empty partys families mysterries

empties pennies mystery peny

SCORE

/8

Lesson 64

Read & Learn	Copy	Cover & Write
discovery		
married		
carried		
religion		
folklore		
custom		
syllable		
fluent		

CIRCLE THE CORRECT SPELLINGS

folklor custom married relliigon

fluent sillable carried discovery

SCORE

/8

Lesson 65

Read & Learn	Copy	Cover & Write
he's		
she's		
didn't		
isn't		
you're		
we're		
they're		
there's		

CIRCLE THE CORRECT SPELLINGS

werr'e you're they're isnt

she's ther's he's didn't

/8

Lesson 66

Read & Learn	Copy	Cover & Write
haven't		
won't		
don't		
climate		
natural		
tools		
comprehend		
wasn't		

CIRCLE THE CORRECT SPELLINGS

tools wont natural havn't

don't comprehend climmate wasn't

SCORE

/ 8

Lesson 67

Read & Learn	Copy	Cover & Write
we'll		
I'll		
he'll		
she'll		
you'll		
they'll		
you've		
they've		

CIRCLE THE CORRECT SPELLINGS

theyve he'll they'll wee'll

I'll shell you'll you've

Lesson 68

Read & Learn	Copy	Cover & Write
I've		
I'd		
we'd		
county		
country		
interaction		
doesn't		
pretty		

CIRCLE THE CORRECT SPELLINGS

state doesnt prety I'd

we'd interacction I've federal

SCORE

/8

Lesson 69

Read & Learn	Copy	Cover & Write
under		
swim		
never		
main		
centre		
border		
fever		
sister		

CIRCLE THE CORRECT SPELLINGS

never mian swimm feever

sister broder under center

SCORE

/8

Lesson 70

Read & Learn	Copy	Cover & Write
whether		
answer		
shower		
sequence		
explorer		
establish		
independence		
passed		

CIRCLE THE CORRECT SPELLINGS

SCORE

establish answer explorrer passed

wether squence shower

/8

Lesson 71

Read & Learn	Copy	Cover & Write
total		
central		
final		
simple		
chuckle		
giggle		
middle		
signal		

CIRCLE THE CORRECT SPELLINGS

SCORE

chuckle simple signle middle

final toal central giggle

/8

Lesson 72

Read & Learn	Copy	Cover & Write
handle		
candle		
uncle		
infer		
prior		
knowledge		
modify		
clarify		

CIRCLE THE CORRECT SPELLINGS

SCORE

knowlege modify handel uncle

infer prior clarify candle

/8

When you have finished this workbook, buy the next one in the series. Scan the QR code with your phone to discover all the Whiz Kid Spelling and Writing Workbooks.

Printed in Great Britain
by Amazon